Wild Travelers

The Story of Animal Migration **Wild Travelers**

George Laycock

Four Winds Press · New York

PHOTO CREDITS

Alaska Department of Fish and Game, p. 12

Bob Brigham, United States National Marine Fisheries Service, p. 87

Andrew H. DuPre, United States Bureau of Sport Fisheries and Wildlife, p. 74

Raymond M. Gilmore, United States National Marine Fisheries Service, p. 67

Luther Goldman, United States Bureau of Sport Fisheries and Wildlife, pp. 59, 89, 90, 95, 101

E. P. Haddon, United States Bureau of Sport Fisheries and Wildlife, p. 62

David Marshall, United States Bureau of Sport Fisheries and Wildlife, pp. 50–51

Karl H. Maslowski, pp. 39, 76, 78

Peter and Stephen Maslowski, p. 65

National Film Board of Canada, p. 71

V. B. Scheffer, United States Bureau of Sport Fisheries and Wildlife, p. 69

J. Schmidt, United States National Marine Fisheries Service, p. 82

Rex Gary Schmidt, United States Bureau of Sport Fisheries and Wildlife, p. 27

United States Bureau of Sport Fisheries and Wildlife, p. 61

United States National Marine Fisheries Service, p. 85

Bob Williams, United States National Marine Fisheries Service, p. 84

All other photographs are by the author.

Library of Congress Cataloging in Publication Data
Laycock, George.
    Wild travelers.
    SUMMARY: Describes the migratory habits of various birds, mammals, reptiles, fish, and insects.
    1.   Animal migration—Juvenile literature.
[1.   Animal migration]   I.   Title
QL754.L36   591.5′2   74–7397
ISBN 0–590–07312–5

Published by Four Winds Press
A Division of Scholastic Magazines, Inc., New York, N.Y.
Copyright © 1974 by George Laycock
All rights reserved
Printed in the United States of America
Library of Congress Catalog Card Number: 74–7397
5 4 3 2 1   74 75 76 77 78

Contents

The Seasons Change

Summer brings a time of plenty for wild creatures in the fields and along the streams. There is warmth and abundant food in this season when the young are born. The red fox raises her family of furry pups in a den on the hillside at the edge of the woods. The woodchuck has its babies in the dark privacy of its burrow. The downy woodpecker carries insects to its growing young, waiting in the half-darkness of their home inside the elm tree. Everywhere reptiles, insects, amphibians, birds, and mammals are rearing their families.

But when the harsh days of winter come to the northern and temperate zones, the wild animals must somehow survive until spring, when they can begin their cycle of life all over again.

Wild animals meet this test of winter in different ways. Throughout the summer the woodchucks have grown roly-poly on alfalfa and clover. In autumn they slip quietly into their cool, dark, underground home, where they snuggle down and begin to doze. Their sleep grows deeper and deeper, and their heartbeat slows. Their body temperature falls; their blood scarcely circulates. The woodchucks are now hibernating, and not until spring returns will they begin to open their eyes again.

Meanwhile, amphibians, reptiles, and millions of cold-blooded invertebrates also hibernate. There is even a bird that hibernates. The poor-will sometimes clings to the face of a cliff in the deserts of the southwestern United States and sleeps there through the cold weather.

But most of the birds in cold or temperate climates face the winter in one of two ways. Birds assured of a constant food supply may be year-round residents of the areas in which they hatch. Among these stationary birds are the dashing red cardinal, little downy woodpecker, screech owl, tufted titmouse, Carolina wren, and bobwhite.

Birds, however, are uniquely equipped for long-distance travel, and millions of them meet the challenge of winter and low food supplies by moving. All their lives they are travelers following unmarked trails through the sky as the seasons change. Consider, for example, the life of the world's best-known duck, the common mallard.

1

Life for the Mallard

The nest was hidden at ground level among the sedges and grasses beside a shallow pond. The brown hen crouched low over her warm eggs, her motionless body hidden in the shadows. Only the sharpest eyes would detect her.

This nesting site had been the mallard hen's choice when she led her flashy, green-headed mate north in the early spring. She formed her nest of grass into a basket just big enough for a mallard sitting on a clutch of eggs, and shaped it to her body. Then she began pulling the little, soft, downy feathers from her own breast, and carefully placed these in the nest to form a luxurious, fluffy mattress for her eggs. The feathers would be insulation; they would help hold the heat of her body around the precious eggs.

Then came long days of idleness; there was little for the hen and her mate to do. Once each day the hen slipped through the grass to the hidden nest beside the pond and placed a new egg on the soft mattress. Gradually her collection of eggs grew, until one day there were a dozen eggs in her nest. Through the following days she stayed on the nest hour after hour, while her mate waited some distance away.

These gulls, photographed near the coast of Alaska, travel with the changing seasons, moving on to new sources of food. Mallard hens are careful to hide their eggs from the view of gulls.

People seldom visited this marsh in Canada's Northwest Territories. The nearest village along the river lay twenty miles downstream. So the little brown duck saw only wild creatures. One frequent visitor was the red fox, who moved along the edge of the pond sniffing at the ground, and then trotted on, as the mallard hen sat low against her nest. No feather on her tense body moved; no motion told the fox where she was. A giant moose sloshed slowly through the shallow water. A mink, wearing its glossy, dark-brown coat, slipped nervously along the edge of the pond, poking its pointed nose into every crevice. Long-legged shorebirds crossed the sky on swift wings. In the distance the duck sometimes glimpsed a hunting bear moving slowly along the shore of the river.

Around the marsh other ducks were incubating their eggs. Summer would pass quickly in the north country, and the young birds must grow strong and be ready to leave with the old travelers ahead of the winter.

For twenty-six days the mallard hen incubated her eggs, leaving the nest only to go to the pond to eat. Each time she left, she would gently arrange the feathers into a blanket, hiding the eggs from the view of ravens, gulls, and other enemies. Then she would move quickly through the grass until she was a safe distance from her nest. If there were no sign of an enemy, she would stand erect and finally lift herself straight into the air on noisy wings, to fly off toward the pond.

One morning the ducklings at last began to pip the shells of their eggs. For several hours the hatching continued, as each duckling shipped away until in one violent movement it managed to crack the shell, then lay helpless and wet, warmed by its mother's body. Gradually their soft, downy coats dried and their eyes opened. They stood up, and one by one peeked out from beneath the female for a first look at their bright, new world.

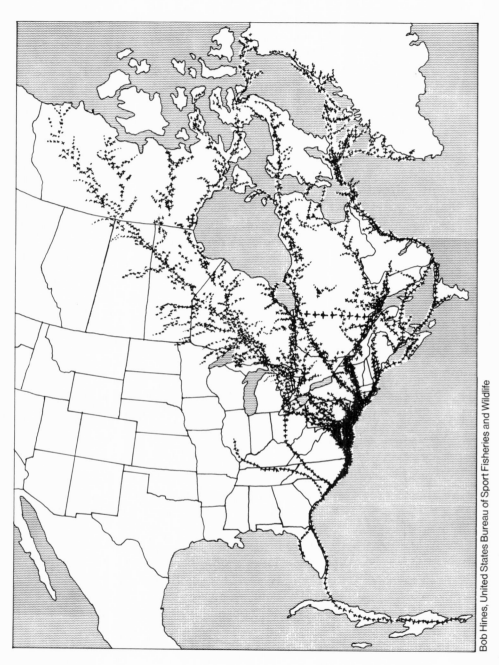

The Atlantic flyway.

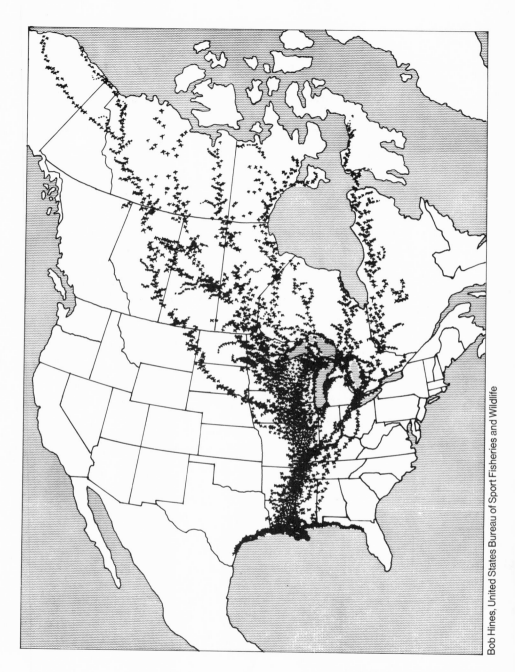

The Mississippi flyway.

Then, the female began to lead them on what would be perhaps the most dangerous trip they would ever take. She must move them to the pond, and they must walk the entire distance because they could not yet fly.

Baby mallards do what they are told. At a warning sound from their mother, they instinctively flatten themselves against the ground to hide motionless in the shadows.

The hen moved off slowly, continually looking all around. Her new ducklings, little, pale-yellow balls of fluff, waddled along behind her. At one point she quacked softly, and instantly every one of them crouched against the ground. For long moments the old female stood very still studying the skies. At such a time her whole family could be destroyed.

Then, surprisingly enough, she left her family. She bounded straight into the air and on pounding wings flew away swiftly toward the pond. Seeing no danger, she returned to a place near her ducklings. At a signal, the young ones started along behind her again.

But the female had not seen the quiet red fox crouched among willow trees. The fox's small eyes watched as the duck flew off toward the pond, then back again, pointing the way to her young ones. The hen cautiously led her brood toward the water. The red fox waited more quietly than ever as the little parade of ducks came into view. But in that instant, a mosquito droned in the fox's face, and he flicked his ear.

The wary, nervous duck uttered a soft warning sound, and her young ones crouched again at the base of the plants. But the old duck moved boldly toward the fox. Then one of her wings began to droop and drag the ground. She flapped about as if her wing were broken. She limped; she floundered on the ground. She looked like a duck so badly injured that a fox could easily catch her.

This was more than the fox could ignore. He lunged from

his hiding place. The distance was short, and he almost caught her, but she fluttered away. The old mallard hen continued to flounder just beyond the fox's reach. He dashed one way, then the other, trying to catch her, and all the time she was leading him farther and farther from her family. In this way she teased the fox into following her for nearly a quarter of a mile across the prairie.

Finally, to the surprise of the fox, the hen's wing appeared healed. With one magnificent leap, she rose into the air and flew away toward the pond. The fox went elsewhere to hunt; and when there was no longer any danger, the duck returned to find her ducklings exactly where she had left them.

On the pond the ducklings ate seeds, bits of plants, and tiny water insects. They fed on the millions of mosquito larvae growing in the quiet parts of their pond. When a hawk cruised over the pond, the little ducklings often sank from sight beneath the water. To keep themselves from bobbing right back to the surface like a cork, they gripped the stems of underwater plants.

The young ducks grew rapidly. Their first feathers began to replace their down when they were still in their third week, and by the time they were two months old, they were completely covered with feathers. Now the young were colored much like their mother. By the time they were six months old, the young males would change from their drab, brown feathers to the rich, full colors of the adult males— glossy green heads and necks, white collars, yellow bills, and rusty breasts.

Meanwhile, the drake that had come north with the young ducks' mother was off with the other males. Their duties were over for the summer, and now they would molt and change their old feathers for new in time for the migration. During these weeks of molting, the males, unable to fly, hid in the reeds and willows.

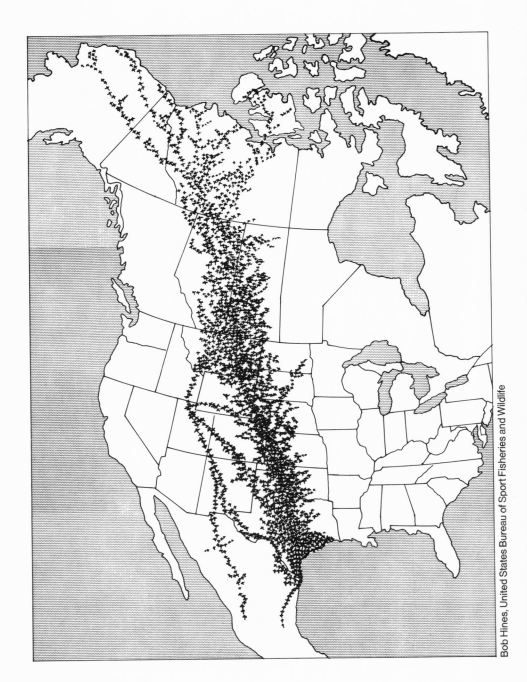

The Central flyway.

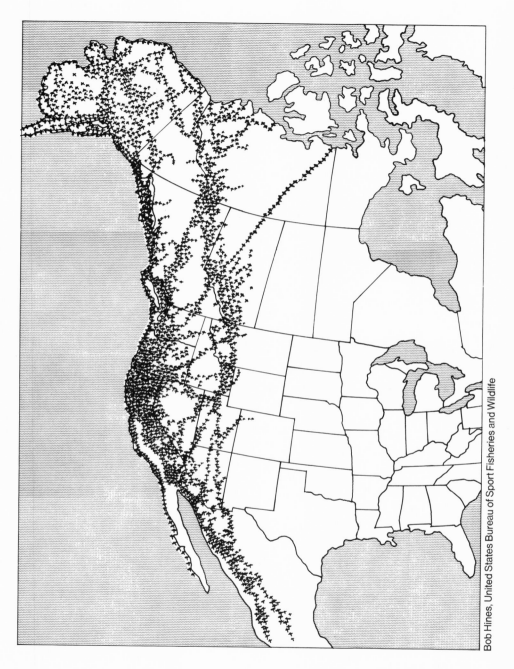

The Pacific flyway.

Winter comes early to the north country. The late summer days grow shorter. Autumn winds carry a new chill across the marshes, and there is the first promise of snow. A strange restlessness settles over the fat waterfowl. Ducks pass back and forth constantly over the marshes, as if practicing to see that all systems are in order for the long trip ahead.

2

The Long Flight

One of the restless ducks is a fine, young male hatched and raised by the hen on the little pond. One morning in October, he rises from the chilling waters, levels off, and flies away from the marsh. But this time, instead of circling back again, he flies on, his wings seeming to grow stronger and stronger. Then new places begin to pass beneath him. He is traveling over strange ponds, little streams, and brown hillsides he has never seen before.

But none of the new places tempts him to stop. He does not know where he is going, or why. He has no idea how long this trip will last, or why he flies only in one direction, toward the southeast. But his course is set, and every new hour finds him forty miles farther away from the northern marsh where he was hatched.

Meanwhile, other mallards have joined him. When he left the home pond, three of his sisters and one of his brothers rose from the water behind him. Less than an hour later three other mallards, flying low, came out of a little valley toward them, banked southward, and joined the young male's group. One of them was an old hen who twice before had made the long trip south.

Ducks assemble in the fall in Tule Lake National Wildlife Refuge in northern California.

At last a lake appeared far ahead, like a thin, blue line on the horizon. The lake grew in size as they neared it. Around its sides broad bands of sedges stood in the shallow waters. Other ducks swimming on the lake raised loud, quacking calls to the passing ducks.

The young male circled back, and the others in his group followed. Only the old female seemed reluctant to drop directly into the middle of the babbling ducks. From somewhere deep in her experience came a warning that frightened her. Long ago, in other years and on other trips, she had learned of danger, and while the younger ducks splashed joyously into the shallow water and began feeding hungrily, the old female circled twice more. Then she, too, came swiftly in, using her tail, half-folded wings, and webbed feet to brake her speed as she touched the surface.

Before daylight the following morning, the young duck was once more in the air. He had set his course through the starry sky and over a land touched with autumn's first cold, gray frost. Most of those he had flown with the day before also joined him now. They flew throughout the last hours of the night, calling often to each other to hold their little flock together.

As evening came again they were still flying steadily along the sky and holding firmly to the same course. The old female was still among them, sometimes taking the lead. Three more strange mallards had joined them during the day.

Late that evening they crossed a quiet, shallow lake hidden like a blue jewel in the deep green forest. Grasses and sedges grew around its shores and in the shallows. On the water there were more than a hundred ducks. These swimming ducks sent their calls to those flying overhead, and the young male circled and flew back. The traveling mallards settled quickly on the lake and began feeding. They stayed on this lake in Saskatchewan for nearly a week.

They might have stayed longer except that one morning they awoke to a changed world. The previous night had cleared with the passing clouds, and the air was bitterly cold. During the night the water had begun to harden into ice, and by daylight the band of ice reached outward beyond the feeding area. The ducks left.

In southern Manitoba farmhouses stood on the edges of square fields; the highway stretched out across the flat country. Ducks were everywhere—passing back and forth between the ponds and lakes, flying high overhead, and riding gently on the ripples of the ponds.

There was one night when the skies were full of pale stars, but ahead of the traveling ducks lay a bank of thin clouds. They flew into it. Half an hour later the clouds had thickened, and what had been light clouds became a sullen, gray blanket. The winds rose and howled around them, and the night grew black. Drops of cold rain pelted the young mallard, and he felt the hard sting of hail as it struck his plumage. The winds seemed to blow first from one direction, then another, and in spite of his strong wings, he was tossed around like a dead leaf.

In the past weeks his built-in compass had guided him. He had never been lost. But now the young mallard could no longer tell directions. All the clues were hidden by the clouds.

He called louder and louder to the other mallards. Sometimes he heard their voices faintly against the howling winds. Then he could hear only the roaring of the wind.

He flew around blindly in the darkness. Then suddenly he was tumbling helplessly through the air, falling to earth. The distance was not great. He pounded against a tree and fell upon the soggy earth with a jarring thud. The pine tree he had flown into stood next to a farmhouse. In the storm the young mallard had seen neither the house nor the tree.

He crouched in the grass, the icy water rising around his feet. Hours later he was still there as the cold, gray dawn began to push back the night. The first light of day revealed a large, square house, an automobile, a tractor, and an old truck—all objects unfamiliar to the mallard.

The wing that had struck the tree seemed whole and strong. He was about to fly away from this place when a large dog came around the corner of the house. The dog, wet and miserable, huddled as closely to the side of the house as he could to protect himself from the bitter wind and the wet snow. Then the dog lifted its head and saw the duck. They were no more than a dozen feet apart. The dog lunged at the young mallard.

In that instant the mallard, quacking loudly, heaved himself into the air again. The dog, rearing up beneath the bird, missed by several inches. The mallard gained speed. Flying low, he traveled nearly two miles before he came to the pond. Several mallards swimming about on the surface called to him, and he settled in to join them. Among them were the mallards that had traveled with him down from the north. Forced to earth by the storm, they too had made their way to the nearby pond.

During the following days the mallards moved on ahead of winter. After leaving the marsh country of Manitoba, they followed the valley of the Missouri River, flying over North Dakota, South Dakota, and Nebraska, and then into Missouri. But they did not stop again for many hours. The young mallard was a strong flier, and some strange urgency drew him along this trail he had never traveled before.

Early one afternoon he saw below him hundreds of ducks swimming about on a broad lake. On other lakes nearby there were even more ducks. His flock swung around and circled back. Tired now from long hours of steady flying, they answered the calls of the mallards below. Then they began settling in among them. This was to be the mallards' last long stop before reaching their wintering grounds.

During their first days on the new lake, the ducks flew out to the smaller ponds and into the nearby farm fields. They fed on corn left behind by the farmers' huge, clattering corn pickers. They dabbled in the shallow waters, filling up on seeds of smartweed and pondweed.

It was during this stop that the young mallard learned about another danger faced by ducks as they move southward in autumn. One night the skies were so dark the ducks could scarcely see each other. A strong, gusty wind blew out of the northwest. When dawn finally arrived, the marsh lay flat and gray beneath low, black clouds.

The young mallard was among the first group of ducks to lift into the sky and fly away from the big refuge lake. The ducks were heading for one of the small ponds some miles away where they had learned to go for their morning meal. Never before had they met any danger on this pond.

The little flock of mallards, flying into the wind, came in fast. The young male saw some other mallards already sitting very quietly on the pond. He had no way of knowing that these were not live birds, but hunters' decoys instead. The decoys drifted on the water near the little pile of brown grass that had been standing on the edge of the pond for several days.

The young mallard was the first to come in for a landing. His feet were down to catch the water and to help him stop. Three other ducks were landing at nearly the same instant. They were still a few feet above the water when two men rose from behind the brown grass. Suddenly the morning was filled with the sound of guns, a new and frightening noise to the young mallard.

The duck on his right tumbled back into the water; another mallard, flying above him, also fell from the sky. But the young male beat his strong wings furiously, trying to gain altitude and to escape from this place. Other shots were fired. One more duck fell to the water. Then the young mallard was away. He banked sharply to the left, flying off as rapidly as his strong wings would carry him.

Across the marsh rolled the sounds of more guns. The little flock with which the young male now flew climbed higher against the gray sky. They circled the marsh and the river bottoms. They inspected other ponds. On some they saw men, either standing in their hunting blinds or wading in the shallow water. Sometimes they spotted dogs splashing in the water. The events of this morning filled the young

The aluminum leg band being placed on the leg of this mallard duck by a waterfowl biologist may later supply clues to the bird's travels if the band is recovered.

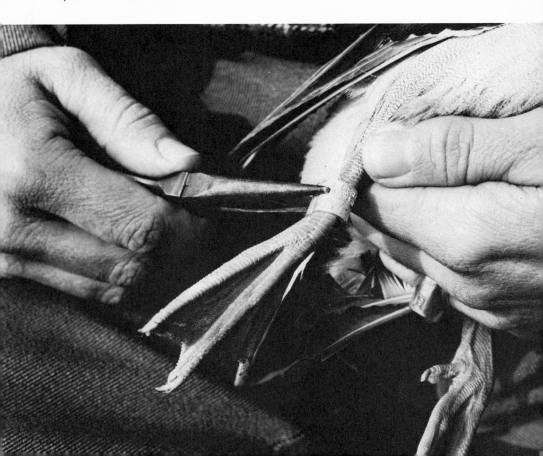

mallard with uneasiness, and he had grown more cautious. He did not find a safe place to feed until nearly noon.

But despite this new danger, the ducks still did not move out of the area. The waters were not yet frozen over, and food was plentiful in and around the big wildlife refuge.

Nearly a month passed. Then, one evening when a bitter, freezing wind swept down from the northwest and the skies were brilliantly clear, the young mallard and his group departed on the last leg of their long autumn journey.

They flew southward and into Arkansas, where there appeared beneath them a small river, its swollen waters brown with mud. This was the Cache River, flowing across eastern Arkansas. Near Stuttgart towering oak trees bordered the streams. Floodwater stood around the roots of these trees. Thousands of ducks were in the woods and feeding hungrily on acorns. Their calls welcomed the little flock led by the young male.

The young mallard's trip from Canada's Northwest Territories to Arkansas had taken him nearly two thousand miles. Other mallards, meanwhile, had flown all the way from Alaska. Still others had hatched in the shallow lakes of southern Canada, the Dakotas, and Minnesota, and then traveled south from these areas. Up and down the continent, the restless ducks had flown from nesting areas to wintering grounds. Some had made only short flights to escape the winter ice. Others, such as the young mallard, made long trips that brought them across mountains, prairies, marshes, rivers, and lakes. For some it was a leisurely trip. Others had covered the distance quickly. But these birds had arrived only to return again with the coming of spring. This is the strange story of the endless travels of migrating birds.

3

Migration's Mysteries

While the mallards are traveling, millions of other wild creatures around the world are also on the move. Land, water, and air are laced with their invisible trails.

Smaller birds—warblers, tanagers, thrushes, and sparrows, among others—are on the wing. Thousands of them pass over our homes and through our villages, seldom noticed. Yet each one is participating in a remarkable, mysterious journey.

Most likely, somewhere the mallard flew over the summer home of a warbler with red and orange splashed on its black wings and back. Colonial settlers named this little bird the "redstart." While the mallards came south just ahead of the ice, the redstarts had left earlier. They had abandoned their little cup-shaped nests, where each mated pair raised four or five young, and had flown until finally they came to the Gulf of Mexico. Then the redstarts, only four-and-a-half inches long, set out to fly more than five hundred miles across the open water without stopping. In this way the redstarts reach Central and South America, where throughout the winter they can find all the insects they need. And when

This thick-billed murre, like the common murre, nests on northern sea cliffs. Some migrate by swimming long distances, while others may not have to travel far from their home cliffs.

spring comes, they are strong and ready again for another trip. They turn back north and fly thousands of miles to the same woods where they nested the summer before.

Migrating birds often fly over the territories of other birds that do not have to travel at all because they have evolved a diet that varies with the changing seasons. The flashy red cardinals that live in the shrubbery around city homes and in the thickets at the edges of forests spend their lives near the places where they were hatched. In summer the cardinals eat insects and fruits, and in winter they live by eating dogwood seeds, smartweed, sumac, and bristle grass.

Another bird that does not travel south for winter is the bobwhite quail. In spring and summer, when its clear, liquid song is heard from the grassy open fields and fence rows, the bobwhite is fattening up and feeding its young on grasshoppers, crickets, caterpillars, spiders, centipedes, snails, and sowbugs. Its young grow rapidly on these foods. But in fall the quail adds more seeds to its diet and feasts on ragweed, lespedeza, beggarweed, and smartweed.

Most other fowl-like birds do not migrate. Pheasants live around the same meadows and marshes the year around. As winter comes, the chicken-sized ruffed grouse of the northern states and Canada moves into the thicker cover of such trees as conifers.

In the far north there is another grouse, the ptarmigan, that does not migrate. Frigid winds sweep across the tundra, and temperatures there drop to fifty degrees or more below zero. But the ptarmigan is insulated with feathers that even cover its feet and turn white to match the snow. In that dark, bitterly cold land, the ptarmigan finds buds to sustain itself through the winter.

There are, however, at least two species of the fowl-like birds that migrate. One is the little brown quail spoken of in the Bible. When the seasons change, it leaves its nesting areas in Europe and Asia and flies south to spend the winter in Africa, traveling at night with thousands of other migrating birds.

Meanwhile, in California's mountains, there is a quail that does not fly as it migrates, but walks instead. The mountain quail, larger than a bobwhite and having a long, graceful plume on the top of its head, leaves in September its high country home, where it has nested and raised its chicks. The mountain quail travel in little groups, hiking for perhaps thirty miles down the slopes of the Sierras in single file. Then, in spring they leave the lower valleys and walk back up the mountain, returning to higher land to nest.

Some birds make only short migrations. One such bird is the song sparrow. Known for its cheerful song, and recognized by the brown streaks and the large brown spots on its breast, the song sparrow may seem not to have departed at all in autumn, for some may still be seen in the weedy fields and woodland edges. But those that are about in winter have probably moved down from the north and taken the places of the summer residents who have shifted a little farther to the south.

It is common for birds to "leapfrog" over others of their species. Those starting their journeys from the far north may pass over the wintering grounds of their southern relatives. The Maryland yellowthroat is a little four-and-a-half-inch-long warbler. The adult male is yellow on its underside and has a bold, black mask across its eyes. The yellowthroats leave their native woodlands in New England in autumn and travel down the east coast. Then they leave the United States and fly over the open ocean to winter in the West Indies. But as they cross Florida, the yellowthroats from New England have passed over other yellowthroats that stay in Florida the year around.

Which birds migrate the greatest distances? Surely some of the runners-up are found among those long-distance champions, the shorebirds. These wetland birds with long,

The white-fronted goose nests in the Arctic tundra,
and then for the winter travels south, where it
can sometimes be seen in large flocks.

This bristle-thighed curlew arrived in the Hawaiian
Islands after flying nonstop for two thousand
miles from its nesting grounds in Alaska.

slender legs go cruising down the continents, often flying in
tight formations, wheeling and turning with the gusts of
wind.

Many shorebirds move north to the Arctic to raise their
young during the brief summer. Then they turn south again.
Nineteen species of shorebirds that nest above the Arctic
Circle spend their winters in South America. Six species of
these tireless travelers fly more than eight thousand miles
between their summer and winter homes.

Among the traveling shorebirds is the ten-inch-long golden
plover. It has black on its underside and golden flecks on its

back and head. The golden plover travels 2,400 miles between South America and one of its nesting areas in Nova Scotia. Does it stop often to rest and eat? No. It makes its journey nonstop, flying over the ocean all the way.

Meanwhile, the golden plovers that have hatched in Alaska start out across the cold, rough, northern waters of the Pacific Ocean toward Hawaii. The young plovers are flying a route they have never used before and are traveling not with the old birds, but alone. Hour after hour they cruise steadily through the skies above the rolling waves until, at last, they see the islands and come to earth to feed and rest from their two-thousand-mile flight.

Meanwhile, the bristle-thighed curlew, a large shorebird with a long, down-turned bill, is traveling the same route, also without stopping. The two-thousand-mile hop to Hawaii is the first stage of its six-thousand-mile trip to Polynesia.

But the world's champion long-distance flier is the Arctic tern, a bird that spends much of its life traveling. The Eskimos see this tern in summer when it is in the Arctic raising its young. Then it sets off on a journey all the way to the Antarctic at the other end of the earth. The Arctic tern's annual round trip may total as much as twenty-five thousand miles, a trip equal to the distance around the earth at the equator.

The shorebirds depart early from the Arctic tundra, during August, one of its finest months, when the days are still long and fields are filled with richly-colored beds of red, yellow, and white flowers. Other birds may linger in the north, as if they do not want to move at all. Some of the late starters are pushed southward, buffeted by the Arctic winds of late September that carry the first icy snows of winter. Bohemian waxwings, feathered in beautiful colors and pointed crests, may scarcely beat the winter storms as they come out of the north. With them may come other late starters, the redpolls and white-winged crossbills.

BREEDING RANGE

WINTER RANGE

This map indicates the distribution and migratory route of the bobolink. Those birds whose breeding range is in the western United States still follow the traditional route to their wintering grounds, avoiding a shortcut across the American Southwest.

Bob Hines, United States Bureau of Sport Fisheries and Wildlife

Some of the smallest birds make amazing migration journeys. The ruby-throated hummingbird, flying on wings that beat so fast they appear to be a blur, skims five hundred miles across the Gulf of Mexico without a stop. Meanwhile, the bobolink leaves its summer home in Canada's open fields and heads southward for Argentina, a trip of seven thousand miles. The spring breeding plumage of the male bobolink, unlike all other North American birds, is dark below and light above.

Among the moving masses of birds are the swift and graceful barn swallows, aerial acrobats with a deep blueback and rust-colored chest. These birds skim their insect meals from the air as they travel nine thousand miles from their summer home in Alaska to the southern part of South America.

A migrating bird may not make the same trip every year. Some may come only as far south as the next food supply. The snowy owl, the ghostly, white giant of the Arctic tundra that lives on rodents, will usually migrate as far as southern Canada, where it cruises about on silent, slow-moving wings that span fifty-five inches. The snowy owl's young, still gray in color, may move farther south. Then a year may come when the rodent supply is scarce. During these harsh winters, the big white owls have been seen as far south as the Gulf of Mexico, where they live well on pigeons and rats. There they may be seen sitting on telephone poles or perching on television antennae. Then, as spring approaches, the owls move back toward their nesting areas in the far north.

4

Strange Migrations

Most migrations in the Northern Hemisphere are south-ward in the fall, then north again in spring. But naturalists have studied the habits of many birds and have found that some, such as the juncos of the Great Smoky Mountains, may not follow this plan at all.

Juncos are members of the sparrow family and are often seen around bird feeders in winter. The dark-eyed junco, sometimes called the "Snowbird," is white underneath while its back, head, and chest are dark blue-gray. This seedeater builds its nest in the northern forests as far as the Arctic Circle and beyond. Then in autumn the junco flies down the continent to its wintering areas, which spread across much of the United States all the way to the Gulf of Mexico.

If you travel through the Great Smokies in winter, you should have no trouble spotting juncos. They live along the edges of weed patches and beside the highways, hopping about on the snow, feeding on the weed seeds. Strangely enough, naturalists have learned that these wintering juncos in the Great Smoky Mountains are of two slightly different subspecies. They look alike and live together in flocks,

The dark-eyed junco breeds in the north and
flies south for the winter. Some, instead of
migrating up across the continent, migrate up and down
the mountains, spending summer nesting in the
high altitudes and winter in the lowlands.

but while some of them have flown hundreds of miles to reach the Great Smokies, others among them have made only short journeys.

By mid-April all the juncos have gone from the valleys. But they have separated into two groups. Many are headed northward across the continent. The rest will travel only ten or twelve miles out of the valleys and up the mountains to spend the summer raising their young in the cooler, higher elevations. This uphill flight takes them into a northern

Great blue herons feed on aquatic species, traveling with the changing seasons to find open waters.

zone and nesting conditions much like those their cousins find in the distant woodlands of the north country.

How do the juncos know which trip to take? They have no choice. Centuries of migration have locked each subspecies into the migration patterns followed by its ancestors. Both migration routes allow the traveling juncos to survive the winters and to make full use of their particular kind of nesting territory.

Meanwhile, halfway around the world, the tiny white-capped water redstart is also migrating up and down the mountains, in this case the long slopes of the Himalaya Mountains. This little bird comes down into the foothills for the winter. Then as spring advances up the slopes, so does the white-capped water redstart. There, sometimes at elevations of sixteen thousand feet above sea level, it builds its nest and raises its young beside the rushing mountain streams.

For both the dark-eyed junco and the white-capped water redstart, these short trips up and down their mountains are true migrations, as surely as are the endless journeys of the speeding shore birds.

Sometimes a bird will take a lengthy trip that seems to make no sense at all. Some years ago naturalists found that young common egrets hatching in southern parts of the United States learn to fly and then promptly leave their nest area. But instead of flying south, they travel north. Late in their first summer they may be seen far from their nests. The young of the blue herons were found to make similar trips, traveling north only to turn around and come back south to their home areas ahead of winter.

Another unusual travel pattern is found among the bald eagles. During the 1940s, Charles L. Broley, a retired banker who had worked and lived all his life in Canada, was spending his winters in Florida. To keep himself busy, Broley became an official bander of young bald eagles. Each year when he reached Florida, he would begin climbing the tallest trees to the eagle nests to place the official aluminum government leg bands on the young eagles. Then if these eagles were found dead, there would be a record of where Broley had banded them and something could be learned about their travels. Broley banded about 1,200 young eagles, more than any other person before or since.

He soon learned from the band returns that some of the young eagles would leave the nest and start out shortly afterwards on long and dangerous summer trips. They traveled northward, up the east coast, as did the egrets and the blue herons. Some of the Florida eagles were found as far north as New England and even into Nova Scotia, a trip of 1,600 miles from their nests where Broley had banded them. Most of them are believed to have returned by winter.

Surprisingly, biologists studying the red-winged blackbirds in the states around the Great Lakes recently discovered that huge flocks of these birds also move northward between July and October. As many as twenty thousand redwings have been seen flying from Catawba Point near Port Clinton, Ohio, out to the north over Lake Erie.

All birds shed their feathers and acquire new ones at least once a year. This process, called molting, is important because it not only gives the birds better weatherproofing to regulate their body heat, but the fresh feathers also help them fly better than they would with tattered and broken ones.

Molting is timed to fit into the cycle of nesting and migration. Most male ducks lose their flight feathers after the nesting period, and for several weeks they cannot fly. Instead, they must hide from predators in thick-growing vegetation. Smaller birds, however, generally change their feathers more gradually and can continue flying while they molt.

In late summer and fall, migrating blackbirds concentrate
in some areas by the hundreds of thousands. If a farmer's
corn is not yet ripe, the blackbirds, mostly redwings
in this photograph, destroy much of his grain. The best
answer to this conflict is for farmers to grow crops
in areas that will not suffer from the bird concentrations.

Famous among the wild migrants are the Canada geese that come down in the fall in long V formations and can be heard calling night or day as they cross far above the countryside.

Some birds, including some species of herons and gulls, make premolting trips to the north. Among the Giant Canada geese, the birds that are not raising young may travel in late summer from the northern part of the United States as far north as the Arctic Circle. There they acquire new feathers before starting southward again ahead of winter. In Europe, members of the southern race of the bean goose make a similar premolt migration into the tundra.

Both these premolting trips and the northward movements of young birds are not true seasonal migrations. The wanderings of the young birds do not become lifetime travel plans, but serve more as a means of dispersing them into areas where they might find new or unoccupied breeding territories.

Oddly enough some migrating birds follow different routes in spring and fall. The subalpine warbler nests in the Mediterranean and winters in tropical Africa. If you were in the Sahara studying birds, you might find these warblers in large numbers during their southward migration. But if you expected to see the same birds coming back in autumn, you would be disappointed, for they return over an entirely different route. Instead of backtracking, the warblers make a large circle or loop in their annual trip.

5

Migration's Hazards

Tragedy comes often to traveling birds. Storms may surprise them, as once happened to the Lapland longspurs in southern Minnesota. The Lapland longspur is a bird about the size of the house sparrow. It nests among brilliant flowers that carpet the Arctic tundra during the brief weeks of summer.

On the night of March 13, 1904, Lapland longspurs lifted from all across the prairies of Iowa and began flying northward. After several hours they reached Minnesota. The night grew darker; snow started to fall and swirled all around the flying birds. Their feathers became heavy with ice and melting snow, which then began to soak through their feathers and chill their bodies. By eleven o'clock that night, thousands of the longspurs were lost and in serious trouble. They began flying blindly into the sides of barns and houses. Some made crash landings onto the icy fields.

How many were lost in this one storm? Dr. Thomas S. Roberts, who later described the catastrophe in his *Birds of Minnesota*, published by the University of Minnesota Press in 1932, was one of the ornithologists who hiked out the next morning to count the dead birds. But there were too many to count. Dead longspurs lay everywhere. There were, however, two small lakes that were frozen over. Here the dead could be counted. On the two square miles of ice covering these lakes lay perhaps 750,000 Lapland longspurs, victims of a single blizzard. Over the countryside around the lakes lay thousands more that could not be counted.

But if they have good living conditions, such small creatures can rebuild their numbers quickly. The following year, in spite of their great loss during migration, the Lapland

Whistling swans migrate in fall to the shallow waters around Lake Erie, Chesapeake Bay and other historic wintering areas.

longspurs coming south for the winter seemed as abundant as ever!

Another danger to migrating birds are strong winds that blow them off their course and sometimes carry them out to sea. Birds may delay their trips when the weather is stormy, but once their journey has begun, only the worst of storms will stop them.

Small migrating birds have been seen to fight head winds so strong that no matter how hard they flew, they were carried backward. Birds migrating over the stormy waters of Lake Erie have been seen to reverse their direction, fly for a while back the way they came, then, when rested, turn back again in their original direction.

Most, but not all, of the smaller migrating birds are nighttime travelers. By traveling in the darkness the seed-eaters and birds that gather insects in the trees and shrubs have their days free to search for food. Even as they feed, they may continue to move gradually through fields and forests, making steady progress in the general direction of their wintering area. Night travel also provides some protection from predators. If night travel has its advantages for the small birds, it also has its deadly hazards, including some new ones birds did not face until recently.

At Eau Claire, Wisconsin, the night of September 18–19, 1963, was overcast, the kind of night on which migrating birds might meet serious trouble. Bird watchers, studying the migrations, had been waiting for large flocks of warblers, thrushes, and vireos. And on this night thousands of birds were on the wing.

One place which might be dangerous for them was the tower at the television station. On a dark night, especially, birds may crash into towers and fall to the ground. Bird watchers from Eau Claire drove out the next morning to see what had happened around the tower. During the night more than 5,500 small birds had been killed by the televi-

Lesser snow geese and Ross geese on their migration route in Oregon.

sion tower. The next night another 4,600 died at the tower. Meanwhile, thousands more were crashing into towers and tall buildings in other cities. These giant steel towers, reaching a thousand feet or more into the skies, are modern threats to birds that have flown along these sky lanes for thousands of years.

Migrating birds have crashed into the Washington Monument, the Empire State Building, and the Statue of Liberty. Sometimes lights on towers only confuse the birds and increase the number of deaths. Thousands of night-flying birds confused by brilliant airport lights fly into the lights, towers, buildings, and cables. But, fortunately, strong lights installed on the Washington Monument almost eliminated the collisions of migrating birds there.

Towers and confusing lights seldom present a problem for birds that migrate by daylight. Daytime travelers include pelicans, loons, hawks, gulls, swallows, swifts, and nighthawks. Some birds, such as ducks, geese, and swans, travel day or night.

Buildings can create tricky crosswinds that come as a complete surprise to the birds. These strange winds may suck birds into an eddy, catch them up in a whirlpool, then fatally dash them against the solid walls of the skyscraper.

Predators have always been a threat to migrating birds. Hawks moving south for the winter take their food from the multitude of birds flying with them. The speeding, little sharp-shinned hawk may take the bluejay for its dinner. The magnificent peregrine, now very rare, picks its dinner from the ducks that fly into its range.

Ice storms and head winds, predators and hunger, towers and lights—all combine to make migration a risky business.

The rare peregrine falcon must travel each autumn from its northern nesting area southward to warmer climates where food is available.

6

How Fast Do Birds Fly?

For many years people only guessed at how fast birds can fly. Some seemed to fly swiftly, others slowly. But there was no accurate way to determine how fast they were flying. Then automobile drivers and airplane pilots began checking the speeds of birds that flew along beside them. Others were clocked flying established distances between two points. Gradually, we began to learn something about the flying speeds of various birds.

Birds have one speed that is an escape speed, a frantic, all-out dash used when they are attempting to escape from a predator. But they cannot keep up such top speeds for long, any more than a track champion could run a cross-country race at the speed of a one-hundred-yard dash. Most of the time, birds do not have to fly so fast. At comfortable speeds some birds can fly for amazing distances, often without stopping to rest or eat.

One such bird is the snow goose, a large, beautiful, graceful bird known by its dark grayish-blue body, its clean white head and neck, and its pink bill, feet, and legs. For many years men listening to the snow geese and watching

The tundra of the Alaskan coast is the summer home
of the emperor goose, which spends its winters
somewhat to the south along the same coast.

Migrating birds sometimes concentrate in large number, as do these swallows in autumn.

them pass across the skies wondered about their mysterious travels. They knew that the snow geese spent their winters in the marshes of southern Louisiana. Then, after years of searching, someone discovered a nesting area of the snow goose on the swampy edge of Baffin Island in northeastern Canada. Others were found nesting farther south along the edge of James Bay, about 1,700 miles from their winter home. Biologists then banded and released some snow geese on James Bay, and subsequently learned that they can make this trip in sixty hours, flying nonstop at about twenty-eight miles an hour.

But some migrating birds often seem in no hurry at all. The black-and-white warbler, a tiny, ground-nesting bird found in the eastern half of North America, migrates an average distance of only about twenty miles a day. This is slow compared to migrating robins that travel along at seventeen to thirty-two miles an hour, song sparrows at seventeen, purple martins at about twenty, and peregrine falcons at an average of thirty-seven. The tiny ruby-throated hummingbird covers *forty-five* to *sixty* miles an hour.

But the flying speed of a bird does not always give a clue to how long it takes to make its trip south or north. A bird may travel every night for a week or more, then stop for several days and nights of feeding and resting. The sparrow-sized, black-headed bunting spends seven days covering the distance between its nesting area in southern Europe and its winter range in India, but it spends five of those nights resting and only two nights traveling.

How a bird divides its travel time may vary from one species to the next, and sometimes from one bird to another within a species. Canada geese, headed north in the spring, pace themselves to keep up with the daily advance of spring. The blackpoll warbler, meanwhile, may poke along at thirty miles a day during the first ten days of May. Then, as if rushing to make up for lost time, it hurries on toward its nesting ground in Alaska, sometimes covering two hundred miles a day until it catches up with spring.

A migrating bird heading back to its nesting area will often travel faster than it did on its trip south in autumn. The wood warblers of northern Germany need only thirty days for their spring migration flight, while their flight in fall stretches over a leisurely sixty-two days. In addition, birds migrating in flocks often travel faster than the birds that fly by themselves. Birds migrating late in the season may also be in more of a hurry than the early starters.

How high do birds fly when they are migrating? For many years scientists did not have much information on this. Then radar began detecting the birds as they flew across the night sky. From this it was learned that most small migrating birds seldom fly more than half a mile above the earth. Bigger birds, however, sometimes fly at altitudes of a mile or more, as do the shorebirds and other fast fliers. The long-legged sandhill crane, cousin of the whooping crane, sometimes flies so high that the flocks can only be seen with binoculars. In Montana, a pilot flying at night once crashed into a flock of swans. These giant, white waterfowl were cruising at eight thousand feet.

Migrating birds fly higher or lower depending on the flying conditions. Cloudy skies will sometimes make them travel closer to the ground. Strong winds may also force them nearer to earth where the wind is less powerful.

The tall, white storks that are famous in Europe migrate all the way to South Africa for the winter, and in the course of this journey they must cross the Strait of Gibraltar. Before they set forth over the water the storks climb far into the sky, so high they are believed to be able to see the other side of the strait. Then, setting their long, broad wings, they glide effortlessly down the sky until they cross eight miles or more of water and reach the edge of Africa.

Among the world's most famous wild travelers
are whooping cranes, photographed here
in their winter area in Texas. They travel
each year back and forth between Texas and
their nesting sites in northern Canada.

7

Mammals That Move

While millions of birds pass back and forth in their mass migrations, some mammals are also moving quietly from place to place with the changing seasons.

The sprawling herds of bison, perhaps sixty million strong, that once grazed North American grasslands were eliminated before scientists could learn much about their life cycles and their travels. But the buffalo are believed by some to have been migratory creatures, plodding over the plains, each herd following a great circular route throughout the year.

It is thought that in spring, a restlessness settled over these shaggy beasts. The old cows that were leaders of their groups would then turn their heads northward and follow the arrival of the new green grass. As they moved across the ridges and along the river valleys, feeding and resting enroute, other lines of bison joined them. Old records tell of herds of moving bison stretching out across the plains for miles. After the bison reached their summer range, once more they spread out, and they did not regroup until autumn, when it was time again for the old females to lead them southward. But no one will ever know for certain whether their travels followed such patterns.

A mammal known to migrate with the seasons, however, is the big, gray-brown elk of the western mountains of North America. If you go in winter to Jackson, a city nestled in the mountains of Wyoming, you may see elk by the thousands. But if you stop at Jackson during the summer, you may not see a single wild elk, for throughout the summer months they are far up in the forests and the alpine meadows. There they raise their calves and fatten on the tender, new grass and shrubs. But in September, with the promise

As wilderness animals, America's native bison roamed
the grasslands by the millions, migrating in seasonal
patterns that took them to new sources of food.

*In the mountainous West, the elk migrate down from
the high country where they have spent the summer
to the more protected valleys for the winter,
and then back again in spring.*

of snow in the air, the elk begin moving out of their summer range. They come together from hundreds of little valleys and move into the National Elk Refuge at Jackson.

In summer, scattered through the mountain wilderness, the elk are wild and will run at the first sight of man. But in winter, in Jackson Hole, tourists can ride close enough to photograph them.

Far to the north, where bitter winds rush across the tundra, the caribou, the wild deer of the Arctic, are also on the move. By August the clouds of mosquitoes and flies have thinned out. No longer must the caribou stand for hours on the ridges while the breezes hold the insects off. Instead, during the late summer season, they can feed and fatten as they wander across the tundra, storing energy against the coming winter.

When winter comes, the caribou wear a new fur coat and also a thick layer of fat. Great bands of caribou come together, as they begin moving southward along the ancient caribou migration routes. They travel about thirty miles a day, walking up and across the hills, swimming the rivers, always moving on, like a broad, living blanket being drawn across the tundra.

This southward movement may take the caribou eight hundred miles or more from the area in which they spent the summer. Eventually, they come to thin stands of stunted trees, the beginning of the northern forests. Here they find softer snow than they would on the open tundra. Through the snow they can detect the strong odor of the lichens on which they live, and they paw the snow away to reach their food.

Do higher temperatures bring the caribou south? No, the land into which they have moved is scarcely warmer than the Arctic plains they left behind. What migration does for the caribou is to take them to their winter food.

Bats that live where winter brings the problems of ice and

snow face this situation in other ways. Many species hang themselves upside down in caves when winter comes and go into the long, deep sleep of hibernation. Some of these bats that winter in caves spread out from the caves for the summer. They may spend the summer months a hundred miles or more from where they wintered, roosting in old buildings or other places that offer protection, before moving back to their caves to hibernate again through the winter. This seasonal migration may be either north and south, or east and west.

Still other species of bats head south with the birds and do not return until spring, when warm weather brings forth the insects on which they live.. There is still much that is not understood about the travels of bats. But in eastern North America live at least three species known to be migrants—the red bat, hoary bat, and silver-haired bat.

Bats of these species may spend their summers in the northern states and southern Canada, then travel for the winter to the southeastern states, especially South Carolina, Georgia, and Florida. They have sometimes landed on ships at sea. There is a record of a red bat banded in Kentucky and later found in Texas, but cautious scientists say it could have made the journey in a load of grain. Others have been found dead at the base of skyscrapers and television towers along with migrating birds that perished when confused in the night by such structures. One naturalist saw a migration of bats pass over Washington, D.C., and reported that the little mammals were traveling in a straight line, sometimes gliding, sometimes flapping, at elevations ranging between one hundred and fifty and four hundred feet above the earth.

Bats that migrate in autumn are usually under way during August, traveling by night, the normal time for bats to be on the wing. Their travels are filled with mysteries which curious naturalists are still working to unravel.

The hoary bat, traveling on long, narrow wings,
makes regular migration flights
between its summer and winter homes.

8

Travelers At Sea

The world's largest mammal is the rare blue whale. One is known to have reached a length of 113.5 feet. These giants make remarkable journeys. During summer months, when the Arctic waters are rich with plankton, the blue whales are in the far north harvesting tons of these tiny organisms. Cruising slowly through the acres of plankton, with its cavernous mouth open, the whale scoops up tons of water. The water then passes through nets of filaments hanging in the whale's jaws which strain out the plankton organisms. The whale's huge tongue forces these masses of food back into its throat before the remaining water runs out at the sides of its mouth.

These and other species of whales may make long migration trips between their feeding grounds and the warm tropical waters where their calves are born. The humpback whale may travel four thousand miles from the Antarctic Ocean to warmer waters around South Africa, Australia, New Zealand, and South America. Whale calves are born without a layer of blubber to keep them warm, and therefore, the warmer waters are probably important to their health and survival.

Along the west coast of North America, the gray whales are famous travelers. They spend the winter and spring months in protected bays on the coast of Baja California, where they give birth to their calves. Then they migrate northward to Arctic waters to feed again.

Another unusual mammal migration begins on the rocky, wave-splashed shores of Alaska's Pribilof Islands in the Bering Sea. The males and females of the hundreds of fur-

The gray whale travels from its summer home
in the Arctic to such southern locations
as Scammon Lagoon, on the coast of
Baja California, to have its young.

bearing seals that live on these islands do not travel together, but have distinctive "his and her" migration routes.

The females and the immature seals leave ahead of winter on a three-thousand-mile-long swim. They migrate

The breeding areas and migration range of the Pribilof fur seals. The male seals move for the winter into the area along the southern coast of Alaska, while the females migrate farther south along the western coast of Canada and the United States.

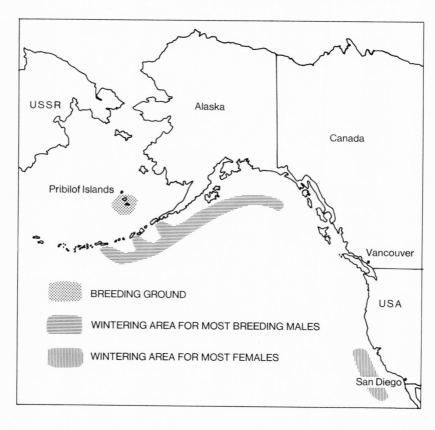

The male Alaska fur seals move for the winter from
the Pribilof Islands of Alaska into the Gulf
of Alaska. The young and the females move much
farther, following the coast to Southern California.

through the rough waters of the Pacific Ocean as far as
Southern California, where the pregnant females spend the
winter. In spring they swim north again, back toward their
islands off the Alaska coast.

Their mates, the old bulls, meanwhile, may have traveled
no more than four hundred or five hundred miles. Instead
of journeying all the way to California, they only move
through the Aleutian Islands and into the Gulf of Alaska for
the winter. When the female seals return to the Pribilofs,

the males are already back on the home island waiting for them.

Shortly after their return in June, the females give birth to their new pups. They spend much time fishing in the ocean, returning every second day to nurse their pups. Meanwhile, the bulls stand guard over the young. The adult males with harems will not eat again until August, when the young seals can catch their own food. Then, after mating, the old bulls go back to the water, and all the seals feed heavily, storing energy for the trips ahead of them.

Across the bitterly cold Arctic the great white bears are also moving, but their travels are still shrouded in mystery. In recent years scientists have attempted to learn some of the details of the polar bear's movements. Traveling in helicopters and dressed in heavy furs, these biologists have searched out the bears that live on the ice packs. Hovering low above a bear, one of the biologists may lean from the helicopter and shoot the animal with a dart that carries a harmless drug. Once it is hit, the bear begins to grow sleepy, and within five to twenty-five minutes it can no longer move.

Now the biologists begin to record as much as they can about the animal. They study its teeth and sometimes place tags on its ears so it can be recognized if found later. Some polar bears have also been equipped with tiny radio transmitters which give off beeps as the animal travels across the ice. These signals can then be picked up by a receiver, and in this manner the polar bear can be followed.

Finally, the biologists weigh the bear before the drug wears off and it revives enough to be dangerous. Though a polar bear may weigh as much as eight hundred or even one thousand pounds, weighing one of these animals is easier than it might seem, provided you use a helicopter. The bear is wrapped in a net which is then hooked to a scale suspended from the helicopter. The helicopter rises slowly until the bear's body is clear of the ice and its weight can be read on the scales.

But even with all these modern devices, scientists still have much to learn about the giant white bears. They live in five countries—Canada, Greenland, Norway, Russia, and the United States (Alaska), and they travel frequently from one country to another by riding on the ice floes. Males travel widely during the mating seasons, and the bears sometimes travel in their search for food. Those living off the coast of Alaska usually move northward in spring and south again in fall, as the Arctic ice pack forms again.

Polar bears of the far north often make long trips
to reach their feeding areas and denning grounds.

9

Migrating Reptiles

Somewhere on the open oceans a giant turtle swims through the waves. She travels steadily, day after day, always in the same direction. Her broad feet serve as paddles that move her two-hundred-pound body through the clear waters.

Once men had no idea where the big sea turtles went in their travels, or even for certain whether or not they migrated. Then scientists began studying the green sea turtles and the other big ocean-going turtles. They tagged them and followed them. A little at a time they began to learn some—but not all—of the green turtle's travel secrets.

The female green turtle must lay her eggs in the warm sands of a tropical beach, far from the pastures of turtle grass on which these giant reptiles feed. Many of the important nesting beaches are in the Caribbean Sea. The green turtle has no choice. It must travel between the two areas, its feeding waters and its nesting beaches.

One of the green turtles' feeding areas lies off the shores of Brazil. At least some of the turtles that feed there travel for nearly a year across the ocean to Ascension Island, a

Biologists working on the Hawaiian Islands National Wildlife Refuge study the green sea turtle and attempt to unravel the story of its travels.

Sea turtles spend most of their lives navigating the open oceans, but to lay their eggs they must return to their nesting beaches.

distance of about 1,400 miles, more than halfway to Africa. Even though Ascension Island is only seven-and-a-half miles long, the migrating turtles find their island in the middle of the ocean and even go to the exact part of the beach where they have nested before. They make this trip every two or three years.

After incubating for forty-eight to seventy days, depending on the temperature, the eggs hatch. Then the young green turtles, about two inches long, scamper down the beach, rushing to escape their predators, and vanish into the ocean. Usually they emerge from the nest at night when they can perhaps escape the notice of gulls and other day-time predators.

How do they spend the following year? Where do they go? These are still mysteries. But a yet greater mystery may be how the turtles find their way. What guides them so surely over the unmarked seas, leading them back and forth between their nesting beaches and their distant feeding grounds?

10

Insects That Migrate

Unlike mammals and birds, insects are not warm-blooded. Their body temperature changes as the temperature around them grows colder or warmer. When winter chills the land, the body temperature of the insects falls lower and lower until they can no longer move. They must either migrate to warmer places ahead of winter or become inactive until their world turns warm again.

Most insects do not migrate. Instead, they hibernate through the winter, in either their adult stage or one of their immature forms. One strange exception is found in the hives of the honeybees, which neither migrate nor hibernate. Instead, the whole colony spends the winter inside the hive clinging closely together in a ball of insects. Those near the center of this mass of bees move and dance about, thereby creating heat to keep them all warm and alive, while the layers of bees farther from the center help hold in the heat. Gradually the bees change places. Those in the center work toward the outside, while those around the outside work their way into the warm center of the colony. In this way they survive the winter.

The adult monarch butterfly, orange and black in color, with a wingspread of about four inches, migrates hundreds of miles before winter comes.

But the famous monarch butterfly, a large orange and black insect with a wingspread of four inches, joins the birds in their migration southward. This butterfly is found throughout the United States. In late summer you may see hundreds of monarch butterflies fluttering over a mountain pass, across the prairies, or along the coast, following the mysterious migration routes of their ancestors.

Monarch butterflies that hatch in southern Canada and the northern part of the United States may travel more than 1,500 miles, sometimes fighting strong winds and rains, to reach warm southern regions before winter. In the East

The breeding grounds and migration routes of the monarch butterfly.

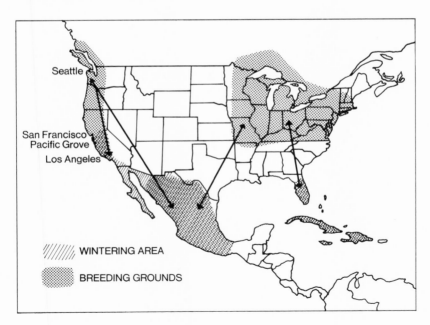

Seattle

San Francisco
Pacific Grove

Los Angeles

////// WINTERING AREA

BREEDING GROUNDS

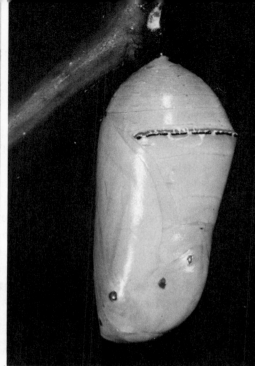

Left. The larva of the monarch butterfly feeds only on the milkweed, where its traveling mother placed her eggs. Right. The larva changes to a pale-green pupa, which hangs from the leaf by a thread. This stage lasts for about twelve days.

they move like millions of shadows, all in the same direction, southwestward toward the Gulf of Mexico. There they live through the winter along the coast in Texas, Mexico, and Florida.

Western monarch butterflies, meanwhile, fly down to Southern California. Pacific Grove, California, is a famous wintering area for these butterflies. Tourists go there to see the big orange and black insects. Pacific Grove residents call their town "Butterfly Town, U.S.A.," and any person caught harming a monarch butterfly may be fined and put in jail.

Monarch butterflies are believed not to live long enough to make their round trip more than once. Those that fly south in the fall must find their own way because there are no older butterflies to guide them. It seems strange, but the western monarchs may cluster each year on the same trees their ancestors rested on the year before, although none of the younger butterflies has ever been there before. Naturalists believe the odor from the male scent glands may still linger on the trees and attract the new generation of monarchs.

In the spring those butterflies that lived through the winter start back northward. They are now getting old, but they have a mission. Each female may carry as many as seven hundred and fifty eggs. These must be placed on the underside of the leaves of the milkweed plant, the only plant on which the larvae will survive.

By the time she has flown north and has laid her eggs, the female is old and her wings are tattered and torn. She soon dies. But behind her there is life in the eggs and the larvae that hatch from them. This new generation of young butterflies lays more eggs. By the end of summer they have produced several generations, and the monarchs have again spread over their range, searching out the milkweed plants, laying their eggs, and rebuilding their numbers. The last generation of summer turns back toward the south and begins a long and dangerous trip that these butterflies have probably never made before and may never make again. One monarch butterfly is known to have migrated 1,870 miles from Toronto, Canada, into Mexico.

Almost certainly, more insects migrate than we know about. In addition to the monarchs, there are about fifty other species of butterflies that are believed to migrate. The "painted lady butterfly" that lives in Europe migrates down across the Mediterranean Sea to Africa for the winter. In spring these butterflies return, following their invisible trail day and night across the open water. Some even travel as far as Iceland, a trip of two thousand miles. Meanwhile, it is believed that some North American "painted ladies" may migrate all the way from their breeding area in western Mexico northeastward to Newfoundland, a distance of three thousand miles!

In the desert country of North Africa and southwestern Asia the locusts migrate, traveling together by the millions. The locusts' travels are matched to seasons of rain and lead them to areas where there is green vegetation for their food. Millions of them moving across the land will destroy fields of crops, leaving famine in their wake. Locusts do not follow a regular pattern of migration, but begin to congregate when large populations of them are faced with drought and starvation. Then clouds of locusts move over the land, each one capable of eating its weight in green crops every day.

Another insect that migrates is the ladybird beetle, a favorite with gardeners because it eats smaller insects. Gardeners sometimes buy ladybird beetles by the thousands because they feed on the aphids which destroy crops. One species in California, the convergent ladybird, spends the summer in the valleys and along the coast. But as winter comes, the convergent ladybirds begin moving up the mountains. There they crowd together, sometimes a mile above sea level, and hibernate in dark places until spring comes and it is time to move, once more, down the mountain.

11

The Migrating Fish

S ome of the most famous of all wildlife travelers are fish. Perhaps the most remarkable of all ocean trips is taken by the American and European eels. These long, slender fish are valued as food in Europe, as well as in parts of North America, and for centuries men wondered where the eels traveled. None were ever found carrying eggs or sperm. Strange guesses were made about the eel's life story. More than two thousand years ago, Aristotle surmised that perhaps the eels sprang as if by magic from the mud. Once the truth was known, it was almost as fantastic as Aristotle's guess.

Life begins for these eels in the Sargasso Sea, near the island of Bermuda. Each egg carries just enough oil to give it a specific gravity that holds it at depths between 1700 and 3300 feet. At this level, the water temperature is between 61 and 63 degrees Fahrenheit, just right for the egg to develop.

From these eggs hatch tiny larvae, transparent and so thin you can read print through their bodies. The warm currents of the Atlantic Ocean carry them along helplessly.

After a year of travel, the larvae have grown to be two and one half to three inches long, and they have changed in form. Now they begin to look like their parents, and they are called "elvers."

When the elvers reach their destination, they crowd into the estuaries at the mouths of the streams, where they stay on the bottom, waiting for the tides to come in. Then, day by day, only the females, it is believed, move upstream with the high tides until they are beyond the tide's reach, and finally they begin swimming upriver against the current. The males stay near the mouths of the streams.

The European fresh-water eel is one of the ocean's great travelers, following a life cycle that was for many years a mystery. Its early travels are in the larval form, but it changes to an elver before leaving the ocean and moving into the fresh-water streams.

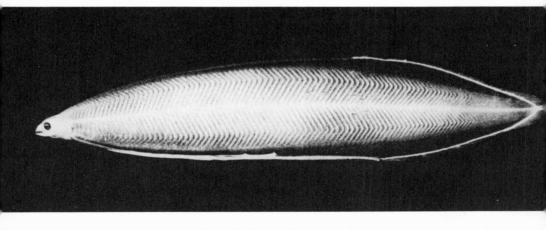

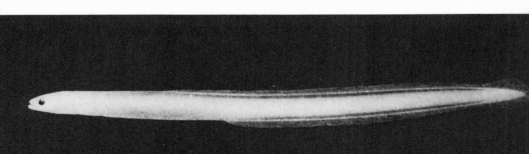

When they are seven or eight years old, the eels begin another remarkable trip. Now the females must migrate down the river to rejoin the males. Then both swim all the way back to the Sargasso Sea to start a new generation. Traveling mostly at night, they follow an unknown route through the sea. It is very mysterious that no adult eel has ever been found between the estuaries and the Sargasso Sea.

But the mysteries of the eel do not end with this trip. Coming into the Sargasso Sea to lay eggs are eels from North America as well as Europe. Tiny larvae from both groups hatch in the same waters. Some must find their way to the estuaries of the American streams from which their parents came. Others move north with them along the coast of North America, but then veer off to cross the North Atlantic Ocean, before coming at last to their own ancestral rivers in Europe. The elvers headed for North American rivers need only one year to make their trip, while those headed for Europe must swim for three years to reach their destination. Meanwhile, the adult eels, having matured and returned to the Sargasso Sea, now die.

Fish such as the eel that return to spawn in salt water are known as *catrodamous* species. However, most of the fish that divide their lives between salt water and fresh return to fresh water to spawn. These are the *anadromous* fish.

Famous among anadromous fish are the salmon. During spring and summer, millions of young Pacific salmon move down the streams of Alaska, British Columbia, and Siberia. They are headed toward the oceans, where they will live for six months to five years, depending on their species.

If these salmon survive all the attacks of their predators, they finally reach their own ancestral stream, which, it is believed, they recognize by odors carried in the water. Each stream is said to have its own odor which results from substances dissolved in it.

There, in their final weeks of life, they begin a strange

Salmon are among the most valuable commercial fish.
They spawn in fresh water, and the young then move
back down the streams and into the ocean, where
they grow to maturity. The mature spawning fish
return to their home streams to lay their eggs.

Alaskan commercial fishermen use a purse seine to capture
salmon that have not yet moved into the streams
to spawn. Biologists determine the numbers that can
safely be taken and still leave enough salmon to spawn.

upstream journey, fighting the current day and night and
struggling over riffles and through rapids.

Finally the female stops and begins clearing a depression
in the stream floor for her eggs. Facing upstream, she fans
her tail back and forth, cleaning the stream bottom and
letting the swift current carry away the sediment and trash.
Into this depression she drops her eggs. By now she has
worn herself thin; her body is weakened. Death is only days
or hours away.

Pacific salmon make but one trip to the spawning stream.
Atlantic salmon, however, may return to the spawning
stream annually for two or three years before they die.

Probably millions of fish have made remarkable trips that
nobody ever knew about. But one silver salmon raised in a
fish hatchery in California must hold some kind of record
for its trip home to its spawning stream. When hatchery
workers scooped up this fish from their tanks, along with

many others like it, they needed fish to stock a stream that runs down from the hills into the Pacific Ocean. They marked all the salmon by notching their fins, so they could be identified if they were ever seen again. From this unfamiliar stream the young salmon swam down into the ocean. Much later, when it was time for the fish to move back into the stream to spawn, however, it did not head for the creek where it was released. Instead it was drawn directly toward the little stream that flows down through the hatchery.

There the salmon met one problem after another. For the first five miles it followed the twisting course of the little stream. Then it came to a highway and a culvert only one-and-a-half feet in diameter. The salmon swam into the darkness of the culvert, still following whatever clues there are that draw the migrating fish back to their home streams. Next it worked its way into a storm sewer, leaped into a still smaller culvert, and then climbed the steep waters up a long flume which led to the hatchery tanks where it had been raised.

Here its journey would appear to end, because above the flume the returning salmon came to a drain pipe carrying water down from the rearing tank. The pipe had a diameter of only four inches, and at one point there was a ninety degree bend in it. Beyond that, the pipe went straight up for two-and-a-half feet, and the top of it was covered with a screen. Not only did the determined salmon make its way up the pipe, but it also knocked the screen covering loose. The amazed hatchery workers found the salmon back in the very tank where it had first lived. They gave this salmon a name. They called it "Indomitable."

Another fish that has a reputation as a long-distance traveler is the "dogfish," a small species of migrating shark. These torpedo-shaped swimmers winter along the coasts of Virginia and the Carolinas. Then they turn north to spend their summers in Labrador. Their round trip keeps them swimming more than 2,500 miles a year, an average of ten miles a day.

What prompts the dogfish to begin its trip? Scientists believe it is probably water temperature and food supply. The dogfish favors water between 42 and 58 degrees Fahrenheit. The changing temperature may be why dogfish sometimes arrive at their wintering waters three weeks later than they did the year before.

Millions of dogfish are caught each year by New England fishermen, who hate these little sharks for two reasons. For one thing, they ruin the fishermen's nets. Secondly, they eat sea trout, bluefish, mackerel, and other fish that fishermen want for themselves.

The dogfish, a small shark, may travel more than 2,500 miles a year. New England fishermen consider this fish a pest because it destroys nets and eats other fish.

12

Studying the Travelers

How do we study the trips wild creatures take? The animals must be tracked sometimes over large bodies of water, often in the darkness, and across wilderness areas. Many people have added information to our knowledge of migrations. Bird watchers have gathered valuable data through their hobby. Scientists have designed remarkable equipment and experiments to help them study migrations.

For example, ornithologists use amplifiers and tape recorders to capture the sounds of birds migrating at night. These sounds can later be studied carefully in the laboratory. The recordings reveal the numbers of birds of various species, their direction of flight, and even the altitude at which they are traveling. Such electronic equipment can detect bird calls out of range of the human ear.

Early in the 1950s, R. J. Newman at the University of Louisiana decided the moon could be used as a lighted stage against which to view the parade of birds traveling through the nights. He set up a 20-power spotting scope and pointed it at the moon. Then he worked out a plan for dividing the moon into numbered parts, like the face of a clock, and

This wood duck was marked with a harmless colored ribbon attached to its neck. A full description of the bird, as well as information on where and when it was banded, were recorded before its release.

This mist net, used for catching birds for banding, was a complete surprise to the indigo bunting caught in it. The bird will be held without harm until released from the net.

designed a method for recording directions traveled by birds flying across the numbered segments of the full moon's yellow face. Since then, hundreds of bird watchers have recorded migrating birds over thousands of hours of moon watching.

Much valuable information about the migrations of birds is also gleaned from banding the birds. The big red brick building near Laurel, Maryland, which houses the United States Government's Bird Banding Laboratory contains more records of migrating birds, in this case computerized records, than can be found anywhere else in the world.

Some two million bird bands a year are sent out of this laboratory. More than two thousand bird banders attach these numbered aluminum bands to the legs of many kinds of birds before turning the birds free again. When one of these bands is found, it is sent back to the Bird Banding Laboratory. There the date of the bird's death and where it was found are recorded. Anyone who mails back a band or its number is sent a report telling when and were the bird wearing that number was banded.

Who are these people that band birds? Most of those who work with waterfowl are trained professional biologists. Smaller birds are often banded by skilled hobbyists who have special permits from the United States Bureau of Sport Fisheries and Wildlife. Bird banding is sometimes a family hobby. One family has banded more than twenty thousand nestling gulls and terns around the Great Lakes.

Bird banding has been going on for more than a hundred years. John J. Audubon, an American ornithologist and naturalist, was probably the first person to band birds in North America. Audubon once found a nest of phoebes, olive-gray, sparrow-sized members of the flycatcher family, on the farm where he lived in Pennsylvania. Would the same birds return the following year? He attached rings of thin silver wire to the legs of the young phoebes. The following spring Audubon found phoebes again among the returning birds, and some were wearing the silver wire he had placed on their legs the year before.

Audubon's pioneering experiment gave him a bit of new information, but to learn much from bird banding, large numbers must be banded. Then the returns begin to solve such riddles as which routes the birds travel and how long their trips take.

This banding of large numbers of birds was first tried in the 1890s in Denmark. H. C. C. Mortensen, a schoolteacher and ornithologist, wanted a way to study the travels of birds. He began with starlings. Mortensen placed on their legs a band with the name of the town where they were trapped. Mortensen was the first to use aluminum for bird bands. This metal is still being used.

A dozen years later, in 1902, near Washington, D.C., Paul Bartsch of the Smithsonian Institution banded 101 black-crowned night herons. About the same time bird banding was starting in Germany. Other countries throughout Europe soon began their own bird banding projects.

In 1920, the United States Biological Survey appointed Frederick C. Lincoln to organize a uniform banding program for North America. As a result of this project, the Canadian Wildlife Service and the U.S. Bureau of Sport Fisheries and Wildlife now use the same kind of bird bands.

As the banding returns built up, Lincoln was able to work out maps of four major waterfowl flyways, general routes by which North American ducks and geese and other birds travel between their wintering and nesting areas. Within the flyways are hundreds of smaller flyways. Some birds cross from one to another, and the flyways overlap. But the flyway idea is useful, especially to authorities who must set the waterfowl hunting seasons.

Banding is not the only way to mark wild migrants. Some biologists, carrying out special research projects, have

This map shows the recovery points where ducks raised in the Yukon Valley of central Alaska were found during fall and winter. Banding information revealed the importance of this Alaska duck-breeding area.

DISTRIBUTION OF DUCKS FROM ALASKA

painted birds with colored dyes so they could be recognized at a distance without having to be caught. They have turned loose green geese, pink gulls, red stilts, and yellow pelicans.

Meanwhile, there is a variety of methods for marking fish. They are sometimes marked by clipping their fins. This is done by removing small fins or notching them. If detected later, for example in fish processing plants, these marks give biologists clues to how far the fish have traveled. Also, there are lightweight plastic or metal tags which may be attached to traveling fish. Or short, barbed plastic markers can be stuck into their backs. Each marker is numbered so that it can be identified later. Another unusual idea for marking fish is to put small metal cylinders in their bodies. Later, in fish processing plants, these little pieces of metal are taken out by magnets as fish pass over the processing line.

But perhaps the strangest of all ideas is to mark fish with living tags, a plan that has been used on salmon in Alaska and Asia. Parasites known to live only in a single river system are placed in young salmon. Later, biologists watch for salmon on the high seas carrying these parasites. When one is found, they can determine the river from which the salmon came.

Even the monarch butterflies are marked so scientists can tell how far they have traveled. During migration they are caught in large numbers from the limbs of trees where they cling for the night and from which they cannot fly until the morning sun warms their bodies. Then a little water-proof, gummed label is attached to the front edge of each butterfly's wing. The label is numbered, and printed on it is an address to which the details should be reported if the monarch is recaptured in its travels.

Tiny radio transmitters can be attached to migrating animals. These give off beeping signals which can be tracked with a receiver. Such transmitters have been used on a wide variety of animals—salmon, grizzly bears, grouse, wild turkeys, songbirds, and waterfowl. Investigators have used airplanes to follow radio-equipped birds. Radio-equipped green sea turtles, grizzly bears, and other animals may even be tracked by a satellite beaming information back to waiting biologists on earth.

During World War II, radar operators began to notice strange shadows dancing across their radar scanners. Ornithologists thought they knew what caused the shadows and they were right—the shadows were made by migrating birds. Following this discovery, radar became one more important way for modern scientists to study migration and unravel some of the stories of the traveling birds.

This display shows some of the different systems for marking migrating wildlife.

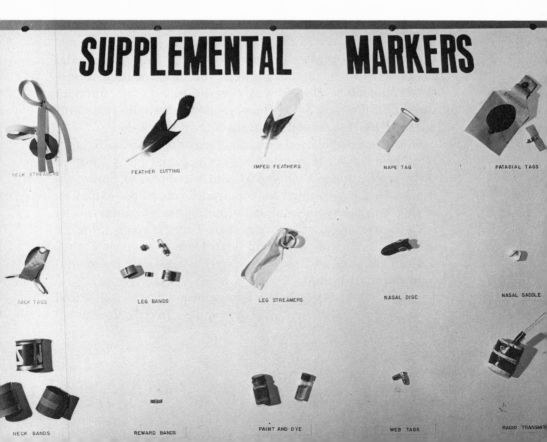

13

When and Where
To Migrate

Of all the unanswered questions about migrations one of the most puzzling is how wild animals know when to begin their trips. One signal for them may be the varying length of the days as the seasons change. Also, it is known that migrating birds store up fat before their flights. And the birds grow restless at night as the time for their migration approaches. Does the answer lie in a combination of these and perhaps other clues? For hundreds of years this question has fascinated naturalists. And it still does.

One thing is believed certain—birds do not usually leave their nesting areas because they are hungry, for most of them are fat when they depart. But the threat of approaching food shortages must have played a role in the evolution of their migratory habits. Furthermore, their seasonal travels keep the species alive over the year. There is room for more of them to live on the earth than there would be if they did not migrate and could live only where they could find food the year around.

Another mystery is how the traveling wild creatures find their way. What is this built-in compass that keeps the eel from getting lost in the middle of the ocean? What guides the green turtles through the sea, the tiny warbler across the continents, the shore birds over the unmarked oceans toward land they cannot see?

Some European warblers were found to spend their winters in Africa, some of them traveling thousands of miles twice a year. Banding showed that a bird, after months of absence and long journeys by night, could return to the same small territory where it had hatched or spent the previous winter. Even young birds who had never made the journey before could find their way as surely as their parents did. In Georgia white-throated sparrows were found to return each winter to the same town they stayed in the winter before, and even to come to the same yard. Somehow they know when to start, which direction to fly, and when to stop.

One scientist noted that the young and old European cranes travel together. Wondering if the young needed to follow their parents in their migrations, he caught some of the young birds and held them in cages until the old birds had gone for the winter. When the young cranes were turned free, they seemed to know exactly what they had to do. Without hesitation, they turned in the correct direction, flew into the skies, and set off on the same pathway their parents had already traveled days before.

Memory of landmarks seen on earlier trips may help some of the wild travelers, especially as they come close to the end of their journey. But most migrating birds do not seem to need the rivers, seacoasts, prevailing winds, or mountain ridges to guide them.

Early in the 1950s, Gustav Kramer of Germany studied his caged starlings in the spring, as the wild starlings were beginning to leave on their migration. He noticed that in spring his starlings all faced to the northeast corner of their cages. Which direction would they fly if they were

The woodcock feeds largely on earthworms, which it obtains by probing in the soft mud with its long, pointed bill. The woodcock winters in the South, along the Atlantic and Gulf Coasts.

free? Northeast, Kramer realized, the same direction they were facing in their cages. Regardless of how he turned the cage, the birds always turned around and faced toward the northeast. From this he decided that starlings must tell directions from the sky.

Next, Kramer built a starling cage on a revolving platform. He fixed the windows so the birds could see nothing but sky. Again, every time the cage turned, so did the starlings, and always toward the northeast as long as the spring migration was under way.

Then Kramer equipped the sides of his starling house with mirrors, which could be adjusted to the right or left. He no longer turned the cage, but only the mirrors, reflecting sunlight to the birds. The starlings were tricked. Instead of turning toward the northeast, they faced what the mirror told them was northeast. Now it was clear to Kramer—the sun helps guide the birds that migrate in the daytime.

But what of the millions of birds that must find their way by night? Another German investigator, E. G. F. Sauer, went to work on this puzzle. For his experiment he used a cage in which he placed lesser whitethroats, garden warblers, and blackcaps. All they could see of the outside world were the stars. And, like Kramer's starlings, these nighttime fliers, during their migration times turned at once in the same direction being followed by their uncaged relatives. What happened on cloudy nights? The birds became confused and unable to tell directions.

Sauer had another plan. He placed his captive birds in a planetarium. There they had only the artificial night sky to watch. But they still took their bearings from the make-believe stars. No matter how the dome was turned, they faced whatever direction the planetarium stars indicated as the right direction for that season.

Scientist Frank C. Bellrose wanted to study the directions mallards fly when turned loose at night. He hauled wild mallards away from their home territories in Illinois and released them at night at distances ranging from eleven to thirty-three miles. How do you tell which way a mallard is traveling through the darkness of night? Bellrose did it by attaching tiny flashlights to the birds' legs. In this way he could follow their trail of light as the mallards tried to find their way home.

Bellrose turned his lighted mallards free on both clear and cloudy nights. Then on a map he drew the direction of flight of each one for its first mile away from the release point. Those turned free when they could see the stars went in the same direction, toward home. But the others, released on cloudy nights, seemed lost. They flew about aimlessly in all directions and were unable to tell which direction was their correct course.

Numerous birds, including pigeons, are famous for their homing ability. Man-o-war birds have served as message carriers between islands in the South Pacific. One Manx shearwater flew 3050 miles to return to its home nesting site, from which it had been air-lifted in a test. It made the trip in twelve and one half days.

During the winter of 1966–1967, Dr. L. Richard Mewaldt, of San José State College, California, shipped 414 white-crowned and golden-crowned sparrows to Baton Rouge, Louisiana, 1,800 miles away. In Baton Rouge, the sparrows were turned free. The following winter, Dr. Mewaldt caught twenty-six of these sparrows back in San José. These birds were believed to have found their spring nesting area in Canada over a strange route, then to have returned to their natural wintering place in California.

Next, Dr. Mewaldt recaught twenty-two of the same sparrows and sent them across the country to Maryland. Six of them were remarkable navigators that completed both trips, returning to San José twice, after first finding their way over strange routes to their northern nesting areas.

Others have said that the earth's magnetic fields may show the birds the way to go home. How they can do this is not yet known. One scientist, trying to figure out how homing pigeons find their way back to their lofts, has tried very hard to get his pigeons lost. He tried every plan he could think of. He even blindfolded pigeons and turned them free far from home, but these pigeons still found their way back.

However, from time to time, birds must adjust their flyway routes to fit new sources of food and changing climates. New food supplies will attract ducks and cause them to

Biologists have learned the travel patterns of Canada geese through banding them.

forego their ancient migration routes and schedules until the food gives out or the water freezes. Geese winging down from the Arctic may stop far short of where their grandparents went for the winter. Some Canada geese once spent their winters along the coastal marshes of Louisiana. Then food was planted to attract them in Missouri, Iowa, and other states to the north, and today only a small number of the geese go back to Louisiana for the winter. For all the wild travelers, migration patterns are not static. The nature of these remarkable trips changes and evolves over the ages.

There is much that is not yet understood about wildlife navigation. But remarkable new facts are being uncovered by scientists. Honeybees are known to navigate by taking their bearing on polarized light. The eyes of the horseshoe crab are capable of detecting light rays not seen by the human eye, including ultraviolet and infrared rays. Polarized light can reveal the true position of the sun, even when the sun is hidden. To get a proper bearing, some animals may need to see only a small patch of sky.

Dr. Karl von Frisch, a famous Austrian biologist, found that the honeybee is capable of telling direction when only a small patch of blue sky is visible on an otherwise cloudy day. No one can be absolutely certain how the bee does this. But von Frisch believed that even if the sun were hidden by clouds, polarized light reflected against a patch of blue sky might tell the honeybee the direction of the sun. The eye of the honeybee, unlike that of man, is believed capable of reading the polarized light rays as they are reflected against the blue sky.

This is important to the honeybee in the gathering of food. By performing a little dance upon its return to the hive, a worker bee reveals to the other bees the flight path that will take them to the food source. But it must have seen the sun's rays before its dance can point out the angle of flight based on the location of the sun and the hive.

14

Home for the Summer

Hundreds of thousands of mallards were spread across the southern wintering grounds. They had survived the perils of lead poisoning, hunger, disease, and the hunting season.

Among the birds was the young mallard that had made the long trip south the previous autumn. He had learned the hazards of the mallard's world. Through the early part of the winter, when there was food in the river bottoms and safety in the wildlife refuges, he had lived a life of idleness. Then by January, changes began occurring within his body. There were glands developing, and he was restless. He became increasingly attentive to the movements of the females. Then he began to flaunt himself before the females. Often he would rise as if standing in the water. He would show off the fine feathering of his colorful breast, and spread his tail, and dip his bill into the water.

To all this the females paid little attention at first. They went on swimming about and left the strutting male to do as he pleased. But gradually the females also began to sense the changes brought on by the approach of the breeding season.

One day, late in February, the young male singled out a female mallard, and for several hours he courted her and displayed for her. Finally, she began nodding her head and bowing to the male. Then, on a morning in early March, the female rose from the pond, and her new mate flew away with her. They did not circle and go to eat as they usually did, but instead continued to fly from the river bottom where they had lived for so many weeks. Their trail lay to the north.

They flew for several hours. Some of the smaller ponds over which they passed were now glazed with ice. Finally they settled into a large lake where they rested and ate.

As spring inched northward, the pair of mallards followed right along behind it. They were traveling faster than they had in the autumn. Sometimes they flew at night, and at other times during the day. Ahead of them lay the nesting grounds which now drew the female like a magnet. Twice during the trip the ducks were caught in blizzards. These late winter storms brought death to old ducks and those weakened by hunger. But the mallard pair had fed well. They were young and healthy birds, with the promise of survival in their strong bodies. Hour on hour they pushed northward, whenever the weather permitted.

Always it was the female that set the course. It was as if she knew exactly where she wanted to go, and the male must come along. They flew back up the valleys that the young male had flown the fall before.

But the female flew on. Ahead the skies were clear, and below the waters were open. The north country called her, and still the male had no choice but to follow. Instead of flying back over South and North Dakota, which the young male had migrated across on his earlier trip, they traveled directly north. The female led him through western Minnesota into new country. Beneath them the farmlands and forests were dotted with hundreds of ponds and lakes. Her route continued on into the flat prairie country. As fast as the thawing would allow, she moved northward. They came one day to a cluster of small ponds in central Manitoba. To the male the little lakes looked much alike; not one of them held any special memories for him.

But one morning in early April, the female led him from the sky onto a small, oddly-shaped pond. The edge of the pond was thick with the brown, dead cattails and sedges of the year before. Only one small corner of the pond was yet free of the ice. This is where the female settled. She had come home, and with her had come a fine, big, green-headed drake.

Not far from the edge of the pond the female built her nest, laid her eggs, and hatched her ducklings. When the time came, all of them would leave this quiet pond which was their summer home. They would migrate down across the continent once more with millions of other wild travelers.

Index